Can We Talk

By
Natalie Harris

Copyright © 2013 by Natalie Harris

CAN WE TALK
by Natalie Harris

Printed in the United States of America

ISBN 9781628392647

All rights reserved solely by the author. The author guarantees all contents are original and do not infringe upon the legal rights of any other person or work. No part of this book may be reproduced in any form without the permission of the author. The views expressed in this book are not necessarily those of the publisher.

www.xulonpress.com

Acknowledgments

This book is dedicated to the assigned ministerial influences in my life that God allowed to play the important role and key factor to persuade me to the next dimension.

Evangelist, Missionary, Beatrice Harris born 1918 – now of the, "Greater New Bethel Missionary Baptist Church", then forwarding to "The Movement of Gods Power Ministries" of Miami, Fla. was my first influence, raise me, taught me, encouraged me to understand that putting God first in everything I do, every place I travel, will get me where I'm trying to go in life. Her term she embedded in me was "Just trust and Believe"

Bishop James Harris; of "The Movement of Gods Power Ministries", Miami, Fla., is my father, teacher, and mentor of the gospel. His life speaks for itself "No Turning Back". Bishop James Harris has played a role in my life since my childhood. Always took time out to help me understand, because he believes in me, I can get the job done. He has traveled with me since 1994 during my evangelistic calling to preach the gospel in season and out of season.

Bishop Jandra Dounveour; New Life Praise and Worship Center; Miami, Fla. one that demonstrated a boldness of faith, endurance, and perseverance, always encouraged me that Natalie, no matter what comes and goes in life "Stay with the lord" and you can't go wrong. She influenced me always whatever you do, step out on **faith not fear**.

The Late Reverend Florence Pratt-Hall; Pratt-Memorial AME church; Miami, Fla. influence me through the holding on to the knowledge of the word of God. Always pursue more knowledge of the word as well as knowledge to further your education. She reminded me always no one can take your knowledge. Gain Knowledge; Knowledge is power.

The Late Pastor Calvin Joyner; A Mission with a New Beginning Church II ; FitzGerald;GA.

A man that played the true role of a father that loved his wife and children. He always encouraged me, believed in me, and embraced the holy spirit in my life. He prepared me that no matter what comes and goes in life always remember that God can do anything but fail.

The Late Pastor Wilfred A. Miller; Mount Vernon Missionary Baptist Church; Miami, Fla. One that played a

Acknowledgments

sacred role in my life, helping me always to understand that on your journey people will come in your life for a reason and maybe just a season, just never let them leave without the affective role you give always ,and that's love. The love that you share is so powerful, don't expect everyone to understand; God knows all things. Pastor Miller have demonstrated a love in my life that will keep me on this journey to continue Gods will for my life. And I best describe him as "The "Conqueror".

Apostle Benjamin and Prophetess Sharon Boykins; True Fellowship Praise and Worship Center; Hollywood, Fla., has played the sacred role of helping me understand, in everything, give God the praise no matter how the road gets. Prophetess help me understand through praise that the devil recognizes where God is taking you in life and if he can shut your mouth from speaking and praising, then you're defeated. These awesome servants encouraged me that when the going get tough, and the tough gets going "SHOUT IT OUT".

Pastor Phyllis Mack; Anointed and Appointed Ministries; Miami, Fla. has played an awesome role in my life from childhood until now. She has influenced my life with her boldness an encouragement to never back down from the enemy, because he understands your stand for Christ. He knows the authority you operate through, so stay on the battle field and put him on the run. Her boldness has encouraged having no fear God is here.

Pastor Theodis and Elect Lady Paulk has played the sacred role of love that they extended during my trying times of staying on the battle field when trouble arise. They have inspired me by loving the "hell out of people", while being steadfast and unmovable in a faith that never failed.

The ministries as follows has also played a dedicated role in my life by allowing me to come in and allow the holy spirit to operate through me to speak, testify, and share life experiences with other women to give them a hope for tomorrow. Special Thanks and Remember "Keep It Moving" The Sisterhood Women Group of the Movement of Gods Power Ministry; Founder Elect Lady Joanne Harris; Miami, FL.

- The Women in Position Ministry; Founder Minister Eloise Humphrey
- Women of Starlight Ministries; Miami, FL.
- Women of the Mt. Vernon Missionary Baptist Church; Miami, FL
- Women of Jefferson Reeves Shelter; Miami, FL
- Women of New Providence Missionary Baptist Church; Miami, FL
- Women of A Mission with a New Beginning; Miami, FL
- Women of Open Door Ministries; Miami, FL
- And to all the other Women Ministries I've traveled and participated on program.

Acknowledgments

Special Thanks and Cudos to all my brothers and sisters of the gospel who thought it not robbery to give me a word from the lord during my trials and tribulations. Thank you for your prayers, thank you for making me laugh when I felt like crying. Thank You, may God continue bless you and keep you on your spiritual journey.

*A Special Appreciation and Thank You to the following businesses that also played a significant role in my life:

- Veteran Affairs CBOC Medical; Hollywood, FL
- Veteran Affairs Medical Center; Miami, FL
- Wrights Funeral Home; Miami, FL
- Hadley-Davis Funeral Home; Miami, FL
- Royal Funeral Home; Miami, FL
- Wing Stop; Miami, FL
- Ashley Stewarts; Miami, FL
- The City of Miami Gardens; Police and Fire Department
- The City of Opa-Locka; Police
- The City of Miramar; Police Department
- The City of Hollywood; Police and Fire Department

Introduction

When reading each chapter of this book, it will give you a wide, inspired, outlook on seeing things, in a deeper way, which are spiritual. Each chapter were written at different times and settings, during which times the holy spirit was revealing mysteries and sometimes indications of how the adversary, the tempter, and the greater one, which is the almighty himself, personally deals with each and every one of us from time to time. I pray that you will understand, and ask God for a deeper understanding of his word and that you may want to become closer to him in order to understand your purpose upon this earth. I pray that you will desire a closer walk with God in order to fulfill your mission that he has designed you to fulfill.

You will learn throughout the different chapters that we serve a, all knowing, loving, and compassionate savior. You will also understand during your journey here on earth, some, things, were destined, when you didn't understand, the many obstacles you've encountered, during that season of your life. You will be inspired by true testimonies given, to maybe give you a hope that brighter days are ahead. I pray that you don't take for granted that every situation that you've encountered at this point in your life, didn't come to overtake you, set you back, or affect you mentally, but each obstacle made you stronger, a better person, or one to understand, to see things differently and in a more positive way, in this life. God reminds us in his word that he will not put no more on us, than we can bare. Remember, if we can acknowledge him in all our ways, he will direct our path.

At any given time while reading, you maybe wondering why I didn't add biblical scriptures, and where to find the written quotations. The word is true, it is written, it's time to walk in the spirit, and it's time to ask, seek, and knock. Throughout the book, the Holy Spirit revealed, that it's time for people to seek God, ask God, and find God, and study to show themselves approved. And if that becomes, difficult, then, pray and find a bible based ministry that offers bible study, with the truth about the true and living God. This will offer the word, not opinions and allusions of what they believe, but what God has to say about the truth of the matter. In order to know where you're going in life, you have to have a destination. Its okay to walk by faith, just remember, faith without works is dead. Understand and remember the promises of God. A promise is a solid decision made, in spite of ups or downs in life; it's a done deal. Be blessed and stay tuned for the best is yet to come.

Table of Contents

Chapter 1   Love At First Sight Came To Past 15

Chapter 2   Seeing Is Believing. 19

Chapter 3   In All Things Give Thanks 25

Chapter 4   Does It Matter. 29

Chapter 5   In Times Like These 33

Chapter 6   Feed Your Dogs 41

Chapter 7   Change Your Thought Pattern 47

Chapter 8   It's Time To Get Dress 53

Chapter 9   Conceal Your Weapon 59

Chapter 10 It was all In the Plan................. 63

Chapter 11 Use Your Tools (Naturally & Spiritually) . 69

Chapter 12 A Fire That Burns The Good 75

Chapter 13 Unconditional Love 79

Chapter 14 Seed and Soil 85

Love At First Sight Came to Past

People often, use the term "love at first sight". When this term is used, it is most commonly used through a feeling. This term is used when someone smiles at another; person, which activates; happiness to get rid of sadness. When beauty captures the unpleasant, it also gives someone a new way of thinking. When some of us begin to understand that love is an act, we can then understand that act; activates. When we think of activation, we will visualize something moving; and when something is moving, we know that there's a stopping point. For those of us who have decided to accept our Lord Jesus, the Christ we should understand in the beginning it was "love at first sight" that cause Adam to become curious about the creation of Eve. Adam recognized that this creation of a woman was different from any other creation of the field. Notice "love at first sight" not only causes us to look and feel, but also be eager to touch. Did it ever occur in your mind that Adam was created and touched with love? When his sight was activated as he saw Eve, he had a different feeling about Eve than the other creation. Well, to help you better understand that, when you have been touched by the creator of love, you begin to see things differently like Adam did. As we know, the rib of Adam was taken by the creator of love and took one of Adam's ribs and placed it inside of Eve, which probably, maybe, or most definitely gave Eve an feeling activating feeling.; Where did this feeling come from? Guess what? The feeling was mutual. Adam, after being created, recognized after Eve was created that she was a part of him, or may I say, has a part of him inside her. After Eve accepted that part of Adam she understood at some point: that "I must listen to Adam". Adam was created for a purpose; and he begins to fulfill his purpose. Another created being named a beast of the field, better known as the serpent, was created for his purpose to "come pass" by Eve, and keep it moving, but he saw someone that was pleasing to his eyes which was Eve. After the serpent began to activate his feeling, which was an act to distracted Eve, he began to speak. In this life as a people we must understand that God created man to speak, declare such a thing, and believe, it shall come to pass. Love at first sight gives some people an option to act or look. Looking can cause some people to wonder, but in most cases the reaction of an act gets things moving. Love can be acted out as a thought, which causes one to react. Depending on the thought, it will allow you to understand the reaction. For example, if someone in your presence is crying, your first reaction would be, "is something wrong?". People often times link tears with pain. And the reaction being is because our eyes tend to see more things that cause painful situations. What we sometimes listen to can also play a negative or positive reaction in our lives. The role that the serpent played; he enjoyed going around being tricky, being a deceiver, telling lies to those who would listen and getting them to react to things that would cause them pain. He caused Eve great pain by deceiving her and causing her to be disobedient to the word of God which was spoken to her and Adam. Now one might think why the serpent would do such a thing. Would it be that the serpent saw the authority that God granted Adam? When God has given you authority to carry out such assignments, you must be careful of that serpent spirit. Eve recognized, but still complimized with the serpent. The serpent asked a question knowing what God said to Adam and Eve. But Eve repeated what God said, not to eat of the fruit from that tree in the midst of the garden; lest you shall surely die, but the serpent said to Eve, you shall not die. So Eve decided to want to know a little more than what God only intended for them to know at that time, found herself going into a situation not by herself but dragging Adam with her also and probably wondering well if I die, we'll die together. Why do people come together so strongly when it's time to do wrong? And find it so hard to come together when it's time to do right. Well in book of genesis the serpent that was made by God was obedient to his creation; than man which was Adam and Eve who were disobedient. God made the serpent more subtle which explains to me he was given a little more because of his obedience, God saw the need to use him for his purpose. In life we must know that we all have a purpose and role if we're obedient. If you're not obedient in your role you can mess up the plan God has for your life. Eve did. She caused God to detour the plan he had for their lives. Notice I said, detour, meaning to, take another turn. Now as a people we must understand that Love at first sight came, to, pass, through Jesus, then the holy spirit, then through us to pass along to others, that we see day by day, hour by hour, minute by minute, so that the serpent doesn't play our spiritual role. In God's plan we all have a role to play. Find your role, it doesn't matter whether you're a saint, sinner, or serpent, be obedient and gain more parts in the play. The creator is the orchestrator, participator and navigator.His love navigates through our lives when all has failed. His love orchestrates our life when we feel like there's no way out. His love participates through the obedient individuals who don't mind activating a feeling that will last forever.

"Remember True Love is the Movement of God's Power"

Seeing Is Believing

    In today's society because of the deception spirit of lies, make believe, and pretending most people find it hard to believe the truth. Now I know you're probably wondering: The truth about what or who? Well, I'm glad you asked.

<u>Example No. 1</u>: If a glass or cup is used for drinking and once you become thirsty, if there's no other dishware in your presence that can be use for the purpose of you needing something to use for drinking, will you stand there and wait for someone to come by and tell you that cup or glass is use for drinking, or will you fill the cup or glass with a SUBSTANCE and begin to utilize what you see the cup or glass is used for. Now in your self conscious mind, because you have seen drinking glasses and cups being used for drinking, you would not wait for someone to say "drink from that cup" you will automatically put the cup in motion. On several occasions while the restaurant waiter or waitress serves their customers, because of

experience knowing what items are used for the purpose of serving, the customer believes the waiter or waitress is experienced enough to serve the right utensils. The customer also believes the experienced cook serves the food at the right temperature with the right seasoning in order to prevent unexpected accidents. Why as a people who say we trust our lord and savior, we believe that he can do anything but fail, we see that we must walk by faith and not by sight, we know that if we walk in obedience, he will grant us the desires of our heart, if we lean not on our own understanding, if we acknowledge him in all our ways he will direct our paths, find it hard to **BELIEVE**. Is it because we have allowed the spirit of deception, "the make believe", to convince us that because we can see things with the human eye, it's no need to walk by faith. People don't be fooled. There is a most commonly used term people often use, "IT IS WHAT IT IS" which means after knowing the truth about a matter. After a cup has been used for so long for drinking and being seen while in use, it's obvious the cup has a purpose.

Example No. 2 : If a person temporarily blind folds an individual, merely covers that persons eyes, then a cup is placed in that persons hand to feel, then asked; to describe this object, the person can quickly identify this is a cup, why because "Seeing is Believing". It is most certain that because the blind folded individual has seen and recognizes the feeling of the cup, automatically believes what the cup is used for. Well it's not only time to see what God is doing in our lives, but believe. Take five minutes or maybe more for the big dreamers, and visualize yourself once in a situation, but in your mind, you've told yourself there is a way out. As a matter of fact, you knew someone else in a similar situation and, some way, somehow, they came out victorious. When people tend to use the mind over the matter they can bring themselves out of captivity, especially the non-beneficial situations which would hinder you in life. Why do some people put their trust in objects, other people, places and non-responding devices? Is it that, we want to stay in control. Bishop James Harris once asked the question during a sermon one Sunday morning, Do you have more confidence in a chair? Why just sit without checking to see if the chair can uphold you. Are you certain the chair will hold you; it's obvious you have more confidence in the chair then God? Wow! We can find ourselves believing in objects. Some people find themselves running away from the truth, and ending up in places wondering how they got there. Some rely on a computerized device such as a GPS, trusting and believing this object will get me where I need to be. Since I see everybody else going that way believing in that object, why not purchase one, not ever realizing, unlike anything man made, a defect can occur. Not to mention God forbid you're on a vacation with the family and decided to totally depend on the GPS and forgot to pray before leaving. Just imagine. If for any reason you find it hard to Believe in your lord and savior; take a few moments per day or night and visualize 1. When you were sick; did you get well? 2. When you needed extra money, it appeared on time. 3. When a loved one was addicted on a controlled substance and prayer changed their life. 4. When one job closed, another job existed. Just think if you can see it, then believe it, then when the opportunity exists, if it's the will of God for your life, go for it. Remember we walk by Faith not by Sight. Faith is the evidence of things hoped for and not seen at that time. Practicing to see through spiritual eyes will give us hope for tomorrow.

Examples:
    See yourself out of debt–(Don't create more)
    See yourself with a better job – (Enroll in school)
    See yourself in a new house – (Take care the old one)
    See yourself married – (Practice Submission)
    See yourself wealthy – (Be creative)

If your heavenly father can see, and believe in you, look in the mirror and recognize whose image, you've been created in. Image is the appearance of an actual person, place or thing. Most time an image is still; not moving which lets us know that something else belongs inside, in order to get the full effect of what the image really is. As Christians we learn that we're created in Christ image. Christ himself asks his disciples, who men say "I AM". As some people in today's society, some feels as though if this image of a person haven't been recognized by great exploits or discovered by something great they did, that in the natural mind unbelieving people tend to go by what they see. For example, it's easy to understand that if I go to a gas station and go inside to pay money to the cashier, she's convinced, that I'm here to fuel up my car. She believes that I'm here for gas instead of everything else around me in the gas station even when I walked up to the register to maybe purchase chips or soda, her question still would be before I leave "Do you need gas"? Now from the spiritual aspect of this scenario, as believers when we go to our heavenly father asking for things we want, we first must believe. When we don't believe, this slows down the process of possession. If my son or daughter comes to me and ask mommy may I have some extra money for a project for school, most likely I would say sure how much do you need, why because I realize that my child needs this extra money for something beneficial to complete an incomplete task in school. If my child didn't believe I would give him or her extra money and would be in doubt of me giving him or her money they wouldn't have come to me. My encouragement to you is, believe in yourself and in the person your ask for what you need. Your heavenly father knows what so ever you need before you even ask. He wants to know can you believe in him enough to give it to you. After you have asked, then ask for patience, being creative takes time, and as most might say "Time is a Terrible thing to Waste". When we were created, our heavenly father took time out to develop a special being like you and I. Then one day he saw that man shall not live by bread alone, but by every word that proceeded out of the mouth of God. It seems as though he believed in what he spoke. When he spoke "Let there Be" guess what? It was. Do you think he had a mind set that "Seeing Is Believing". Please by all means continue to walk by faith, so that the promises will be manifested right before your eyes.

In All Things Give Thanks

When we as a people learn to know that giving thanks can benefit us more than harming us, we'll realize why we were created. For some of us who don't believe, we don't realize we make it hard to receive. Believe what? Receive what? Glad you asked. When we learn that in spite of situations or circumstances, giving thanks can advance, the process of what you're believing God for. Thanking your heavenly father can get prayers answered on time. Notice I said, on time. Thanking your parents for things they could or could not afford to give you, enables them to eagerly do more. Thanking your husband or wife for the simple things each one performs creates a stronger foundation of love to be expressed. Thanking your children causes them to think twice before making wrong decisions. Thanking your boss gives him or her a mind set to consider you for a promotion someday. Being thankful helps us to realize, that matters can be worse. In todays society it has been misunderstood that we must be thankful for the good always. But what about being thankful for some of the bad. As Christians we quote "All

Things Work Together for Those that Love the Lord". But do we really know what that mean? Let's take a moment and stroll down memory lane. Giving thanks when bad weather arose helps people drive more cautiously, why because on a bright sunny day, people tend to speed, run stop signs, lights or maybe strike a pedestrian and keep riding. Giving thanks through bad relationships develops strength, endurance, patients and better attitudes. Giving thanks when your loved one has made a mistake brings better understanding and communication skills. Giving thanks while bills are overdue and continuously palling up with no extra money to pay them, helps us to trust God when will can't trace him. It also helps us think before we spend un necessary money at that moment. Unlike some of us we spend out of hurt, pain, shame, and embarrassment to cover the unexplainable emotions we go through. Giving thanks to things that happen to us in life, we didn't expect or didn't deserve helps us to realize that were not perfect, and if we continue by faith we will get to a place of perfection. Giving thanks when some people committed a crime and spending time in prison gave them a total new outlook on life, which in time developed them to become who they are today. Being in prison for some individuals gives them a reality check. Giving thanks when mama says "No you can't go outside to play today, get in the kitchen and learn something, developed, great Chefs. Giving thanks for having the will power to "Say No" to drugs and alcohol extends a long and healthier life. Being thankful releases happiness, joy, peace and love, even when there's kaos , confusion, an negativity all around us. When there's barely enough money in the bank; give thanks and expect the money to come some way, somehow, just know that it's on the way. When husband, wife, children, boss or car is acting up, give thanks and watch the turn around. Little Johnny may come home someday and say mommy guess what I'm tired of smoking, drugs are not for me. I love me today. Husband will also come home someday and confess "Honey I Love You" and I can't afford to lose you "I promise I will be that husband you married years ago; I will be that father to the children, I will work hard and take care my family the way God says a husband must love his wife; thank you honey for not giving up on me. The wife will begin to cook more, spending less time on the telephone, discussing nothing beneficial , she will say to her children, I apologize for being angry with your father; I will be a better mother and humble myself to be a better housekeeper, thank you for putting up with me, when at times I felt like giving up. The boss might walk in at work someday and say "I know it haven't been easy" working under pressure. The higher ups have been on me about something that I've been on you, which was stupid. I apologize for pressuring you when I was under pressure, and all you did was continue to smile reminding me that everything was going to be alright, and you continued to work in spite of. Please by all means I feel you have proven yourself worthy of handling this position when I retire, will you except this promotion, I believe the department will blossom with your creative ideas, skills, and great customer service you perform; will you except? you deserve it, and thank you for being so tolerant. So remember giving thanks in all things can make a difference. Continue to give thanks no matter how it looks, no matter how it feels because anything good is worth being thankful for.

Be Thankful

Does It Matter?

In todays society some people say our lord and savior was black, some say he was white, some say he was a gentile, some say he was a Jew. My question is "Does it Matter"? When Christ looks at us he doesn't see race, color, or creed, he recognizes the hearts of men, women and children. If we believe we have been created in his image, then, does it matter who God uses, to love you, take care of you, bless you. Sometimes in life we as a people can hold or I might say, delay the movement of gods power in our lives by how we think or act. When God was ready to destroy creation his son said to him, father, have mercy on them for they know not what they do, meaning spare their lives, they don't realize who their doing it to, they don't realize, the Love I have for them. They don't understand I gave up my life, so that they can have a chance in life. ? When someone is willing to give up their desires to make another happy, that's Love. Giving up things, people, and places that you enjoy; which may not be beneficial, depending on the type of people, places, or things, just to make that ultimate sacrifice, so that one who cares nothing about themselves or live in general can be difficult not knowing is it worth it. Does it matter if you don't Love me, but I continue to love you. Why should I discontinue such a wonderful feeling of how I want to be treated; just because you don't understand how to live, love, and laugh. In todays society we have to be careful not to allow negative thinking people, cause us to act in ways that are not positive. This can create images that don't exist. Who wants to live a lie? In most relationships today people sometimes get intimated by who's making the most money in the household, driving the finest vehicle, or maybe just a beautiful person inside out, Does it matter? It's all going to one place, If we say we as one, together we stand. It's obvious the most common thing to do today is get a divorce, let's separate, take half, and go your way. Why do we find it much easier to separate? It's obvious someone in the relationship has inner fears, struggles, or maybe just don't care. Most time some people get caught up worrying about being validated by others. My question is "Does it Matter". If we as a people spend the majority of our life concerned about how others see us, instead of being concerned about how we see ourselves, most times life can pass you by. Does it Matter if I'm white, black, cacacion, Indian, short, tall, skinny, oversized or medium built. What matters is, how I see myself. Some people are happy with themselves, just the way they are, and most times when it's that way, they can be adjustable; they will make changes to make another person happy. Nevertheless an unhappy person will always find

Does It Matter?

something to use to justify why their unhappy and expect others to pacify their feelings. Does it matter if you've had an unhappy past, and now, God has brought them to where they are today. That can be a good thing, If one can take the positives and leave the negatives. It's the negatives of the past that delays the future. Ask yourself does it matter, what, I've lost in my past, what's important is ,while I took the loss, the gain still excepted me, "I'm still here".

Remember always, what matters

In Times Like These

At the moment of disappointment, distress, distraction, delusion, and difficult times, the adversary (the devil) has away of conditioning your mind to believe what he presents is true. Remember, in times like these, one must stand firmly on their foundational beliefs, understanding by faith, your current situations that's causing you grief, sorrow, pain, and agony will change. In the natural mind people tend to believe what they see with the human eye. When looking through spiritual eyes the mind tends to go beyond the current image. For example: In today's society our youth understands that in times like these, living in poverty, unemployed, no, or little education causes them to use the term most frequently "I got to do, what I got to do" meaning, any means necessary I will survive. Because of some them looking through the natural eye they feel let me express myself, nobody cares, nobody recognizes what I can do, they express their art work on the walls of the inner city with graffiti, they act out the clever way of robbing banks, other individuals, and company budgets, just to prove they can get the job done. Now if someone spiritual, with a spiritual insight help them understand that, their hands are gifted to become someday a great artist, an Euterprenual, one that can build businesses, companies to create more jobs for their community. But in times like these some people who have developed a spirit of greed allow some of our talented, brilliant minded, children today, use what they have to generate billions of dollars, just to go in the pockets of those who don't care about anyone but themselves. They create some video games, which displays nothing but terror, ways of robbing, stealing and killing. But once some of our children today come in contact with the demonic forces of acting out the game they play, then the society begin to look at them like they've done so much wrong. Until we as a people, get back to teaching them the foundation of obeying the laws of the land, the chaos will continue. In times like these, fathers, mothers, leaders must come together in order to take back a generation from the adversary (the devil). I f we say we have the victory and the devil is defeated, then we need to act like it. Communication, is the number one tool to get started. In times like these husbands and wives must get on one mind, in order to fulfill the plan of holy matrimony and demonstrate the family structure around the children, in order for them to know how someday, not to allow the devil to enter in the family. In times like these children must understand that they shall live and not die by un necessary foolish mistakes, bad relationships, peer pressure, and misleading teachings, so that if they obey their parents, their days will be longer upon this earth. In times like these spiritual leaders must stand firmly on the word, getting pass, envy, jealously, backbiting, competiveness, religious spirits, tailor made doctrines, false prophecies, and other man made, make beliefs in order to convince themselves this is the way. In times like these education seems to be talked about being at the top of the list, nevertheless it appears to be at the bottom when casinos, lottery, and quick picks, were voted in and are receiving the most attention when it comes to are children's education. It's sad when teachers took time out and decided to choose a career which is needed to build a better future, for not only the children, but a better society, now finding themselves in the middle of chaos, due to a miss management of funds, that was once decided after voting, allocated for the purpose of education. It's obvious in times like these the adversary really knows how to get in, and fit in. Why? Because as a people we allow our selfish, greedy hunger for money cause us to do things that we know that's not beneficial to ourselves and no one else. In times like these people must understand that in order to walk in the divine revelation of what God intended for people to recognize the image they were created in, will give them a better understanding of their purpose for life. Some scientists believe that the world is operating by gravity, pressure, and movement alone. This mind set can cause a minimal level of thinking. Being created in the image, of one that holds all power in his hands, convinces me to realize that, after man was created, and life was blown in the nostrils of man, we are not just any creature. In times like these we must understand there will be a constant battle going on, here on earth, leaving people with a mind set of several beliefs. If as a people we can learn to go beyond our natural mind set, and create beneficial thoughts, rather than thoughts that takes us into captivity and bondage, we will find ourselves living a more healthier and prosperous life. It's obvious in times like these the adversary knows when, where, and how to attack Gods people. For example: Richard Harris enrolls himself in college committing himself to 2 years of education as a certified Automotive Technologist. He faithfully gets up daily to get to school on time. On Fridays one of his courses requires him to take a class on – line. Richard has made it to the finalization of his class this final semester, 90 days away from his targeted graduation date, then to discover his home computer Laptop crashed. Because the adversary recognizes, Richard will be graduating within 90 days, he sends a spirit of delay. Now in times like these in order for Richard to accomplish his goal, he can't allow the spirit of delay, to hold him back. I replied ! any means necessary, thank God for the library or Auntie Joanne. In times like these as a people we must help others recognize the different spirits in operation in order to accomplish goals we set in life and when walking with God. The spirit of distraction has creaped in this generation keeping them focused on electrical computerized devices such as cell phones, computers, gps systems, and video games. If these items are not used in a beneficial way, they can become hazardous to our health. Yes, I meant Hazardous to our health. I know you're probably wondering how so? Well I'm glad you thinking with the natural mind and not relying on each time you need to express yourself, you rather depend on a device, instead of face to face. For example: Andrea and Bernard enjoys the operational mode of computerized devices. Any means necessary they have became experts with no intense instructions. Just one day, allowed their fingers to do the walking and talking. As strange as this may sound, a spirit of distraction creeped in and cause Andrea to get off focus from the needful purpose of a cell phone, and computer, by not communicating with a person face to face. Which now, caused her to become very bashful and shy, holding her back from the the creative mind she holds to expressing her talents when needed openly. On the other hand, Bernard is captured by what he visualizes, on his video games, which causes mood swings, when he's disturb at the time of accomplishing his goals, getting to the highest level the game can offer. In times like these, some people must gain self control, respect, and knowledge of today's general way of communicating. Some devices can be used for the good, but once the adversary (the devil) entered in these same devices can be used against us. For example: A GPS car system device is very helpful when traveling. It is used to track road directions, weather, and traffic conditions which simply means most times, I don't know where I'm going; I'm lost. When the adversary recognizes we're lost, he enters in with the spirit of fear, frustration, and anger which is bad for our HEALTH, which now brings on high blood pressure, anxiety attacks, and headaches. When police use these similar devices against us then we wonder, whom ever invented such a device, had to have some good and bad on their mind. It times like these if we as a people don't grasp the foundation of putting God first and allowing the holy spirit to lead a guide us, we might find ourselves making life more difficult then God really intended for us to live. In times like these we must learn to follow instructions. Because God all knowing and for seeing that after the fall of man, creation could end up in a chaotic state. He told Adam, eve, and the serpent what they will do for the rest of their lives because of disobedience. In times like these if the law requires us to do things a certain way, we must abide by the rules.

For Example: John was given specific instructions how to master a task that will be beneficial to generations to come. He being the master of brilliant mind sets, teaching people the way he see things only, allowed him to take turn from the specific instruction given, cause him to spend the rest of his life in jail. Why? because along the way, emotions, pride, greed, and miss directing the people eventually reminded him, "I didn't follow instructions". In times like these the adversary has a way of causing us to see things in a "positive lime light", meaning a bitter in end, portraying, that his way is better. If we don't pray and ask God for the spirit of discernment, and wisdom we could find ourselves in dangerous situations.

In Times Like These

In times like we can't allow what we think all the time cause us to make rational decisions, especially if we fail each time we go at it. In time like these sometimes getting a second opinion can reassure you the first decision you're about to make will be definite. In times like these if we don't learn and to practice watch, watch, watch, listen as well as pray, some situations can be avoided or maybe save your life.

Bishop James Harris once said, "If you don't stand for something, you'll fall for anything. So in times like these, stand on the foundation of the true and living God, believe through his son, and allow the holy spirit to lead and guide you into to all truth, because in times like these the battles of life, might take you down or take you under.

Continue to Watch, Watch, Listen,
as well as Pray

Feed Your Dog

Part One

Most young people today often use the term "My Dog". While using this term they greet each other by saying "What's up Dog", "Yo Dog" , "Later Dog". Approaching each other, in that manner, gives them the mind set, that, that's, their hommie or friend and their, either, okay with that person or could maybe at times get into a misunderstanding. After analyzing multiple slang words use in todays society, I found this slang to be very interesting. Knowing that everyone have their own way of communication, using the term "Dog" as an approach can cause doors to be open for greeting an individual or demonic spirits to creep in. The holy spirit revealed to me when the term "A dog is a man's best friend" is used its because maybe they have something in common. When the term What's up dog is used, what are you getting into, clearly lets us know that their in agreement, to get into the same thing. When a certain dog gets into a certain situation, that dog already have an instinct on how to attack, if the case maybe. Until that dog is trained to do a certain thing, that dog will maintain the attributes of a dog. Once a dog has been humanly trained by a human, then the dog began to develop human attributes. For Example: Until a dog is trained to play (showing love), attack (biting), to hear (watching and listening), the more the dog is trained, the awareness you'll discover. So from the world to wisdom, we must train the New Generation to understand when they begin to take on the attributes of a dog, they will find themselves doing doggy dog things. We must help them, love them, and train our children today, to realize how to recognize demonic spirits. We must show them how not to open their spiritual gates which is their eyes, ears, mouth, and their minds to things that will harm them. Remember their still babes. Until babies are fully developed, there are at stages during growth. Since now we understand, what this generation needs today, lets help them "feed their dogs" (friends),the one that means so much to them. As parents, teachers, mentors, leaders, whatever role we can play in our children lives today, we must take time out and explain to them what's going on with them spiritually as well as in the natural. But in order for us to do this, we as parents must get in a place, to be that example. We can do this by continuing to pray, mentoring, and reaching out to them in areas we find they are weak in. We as parents have to pay more attention to what spirit is in operation. When that spirit is recognized, we can attack that spirit by praying and calling out that spirit out, and sending it to a dry place. Always remember when you're called to do something, you will be sent to do it. Satan knows this and

Feed Your Dog

he has no hesitation in getting the job done. Once we as parents begin to feed our children with Unconditional Love, we will begin reaching others, that maybe following the attributes of that untrained, vicious dog that only looks for something to eat and destroy. Our children are not dogs, their created in the image of Christ, for those that believe. Now since they have open their souls to receive that he's my friend, that's my dog, Let's feed their dogs. I know you're probably wondering how can I do that, well you'll find a MENU in part II of this chapter, and please by all means follow instructions given in order to get results. Remember in order for a good meal to come out right, you must follow the instructions of the recipe. Some attributes of the vicious dog traveled through the generational bloodline. If daddy, uncle, cousin, son, or nephew, allowed themselves to indulge in such things as X-rated movies, pornogryfy, strip clubs, and orgies, they didn't realize they opened their soul and spirit to vicious attacks, that if they can't perform the way they were introduced to such performance they will begin to go outside into society with that same hunger, to hunt, to attack or maybe kill. So it's very important for us as parents and our children not to indulge in such activities. In today's society we complain about being debt free, or the economy but we can began driving poverty out of our lives by, not fulfilling the lust of the flesh. Not becoming the vicious dog by indulging in unnecessary activates that may cause harm or death in a long run. A good dog after being well trained knows how to control anger, attack, when necessary and protect his keeper. In order for a well-trained dog to be useful, that dog is trained to first listen. If this generation today is not taught to listen, before given instructions, disaster can easily surface.

Part II *Menu*: INSTRUCTIONS:

Notice attitude changes when or if this happens to a loved one who has come in contact with an unusual spirit. Pray immediately a least 7 days between 3:00am – 4:00am. Sacrifice and discipline will be needed in order to gain results.

(Fastening) will need to be included from 6:00am – 6:00pm, partial or complete. Partial may consist of fruits ,vegetables and water; or complete consists of water only. The main key is to believe and expect, once you've followed specific instructions. Don't ask questions, only give words of encouragement, be supportive to anything positive, your loved one may ask, this confuses that spirit. That spirit and most demonic spirits are in operation at the above time.

When you open your mouth, begin praying, calling out that spirit, then send that spirit to a dry place. Demonic spirits can only operate once they've entered into a human being. Because demonic spirits operate at their best through flesh, please don't allow your flesh to become weak, begin thinking positive, stay focus, feed your spirit, starve your doubt.

After that, seal your prayer, with the changes you want to see take place in your loved ones life. Then begin to give God praise for the manifestation of the change. Remember if you don't seal your prayer, you'll leave a door open for other spirits to creep in. With your Love, one will change in one area, then begin failing in another area. Strive for wholeness, completeness, the total man 100 % needs to come forth in order to move forward successfully. Because this generation uses the term "My Dog" (their friend), tell them you're praying for their friends; that's when you'll see the changes in your loved one's life, and guess what, when the change occurs, in their friends life, they'll come back to you and respond, thanks mom or dad, my friend was about to or got into some trouble and I remembered you told me you're praying for my friends, that's when they will begin to "FEED their DOGS" (teach their friends). Remember it's our job to remind our children what the word of God declares. The book of proverbs will give them and help them through life. Warnings and a way out are needed in these last and evil days. Get creative when giving them a scripture. Create family time and discuss the latest confession, the latest battle, their friend maybe had or going through. Be helpful. Example: One of their hommies or dogs went to jail, help your loved one to understand his dog has been locked up temporarily, until he gain some self-control to be obedient to the laws of the land, and there's a price to pay when you don't obey. Bonding their hommies out of jail is not the answer. By no offence for some people a cage can be used to, protect, prevent, and promote self-control. So to all caring parents, leaders, friends, and most all hommies.

Remember, "Feed Your
Dog the right food"

Change Your Thought Pattern

The enemy, the adversary, the liar, the deceiver, (the devil) has one job left while he's here on earth, and that is to steal, kill, and destroy. My question is will a man rob God? How? Well, we know that the bible declares, through tithes and offerings. For some of those who don't understand the power of giving, the adversary have already put you in a mode of fear, which is a trick to keep you from prospering. If God <u>gave</u> his only begotten son, it's obvious giving is important. When you began to sow your tithes and offerings in the kingdom of God, three things instantly takes place, 1. The word declares the lord will rebuke the devour, meaning to stop something that was about to be said or happen to you or your finances. 2. The windows of heaven will open and pour out blessings, you won't have enough room to receive. 3. He will cause men to give unto your bosom. Quick testimony and word of advice, as a single parent mother while trying to survive a put my child through college, with not enough money to pay the bills, I found myself being obedient to the word of God. In addition to paying my tithes and an offering, I secretly sowed into someone else child while he was in college. At that time I really was unable to afford to make that move, but knowing and believing Gods word, and knowing that one day I desired my child to go to college someday, I found that, what you do in secret God will reward you openly. My child has completed 2 years college, and it didn't cost him anything but perseverance, lots of studying, and staying focus. The lord really rewarded me openly by letting me know, the importance of giving. When we as a people learn how to give, we will rebuke Satan from coming in trying to kill, steal, and destroy the things God is trying to give us. In order to get the things in life release to you that God promise, it starts by giving. The bible clearly lets us know, we must render our reasonable service. To render means to give it up, hand it over; or to serve. Because of the lack of knowledge, people are being defeated and bound by Satan. If he recognizes how to possess the promises of God, shouldn't we as a people take the time to really know God for ourselves. This is why it seems that Satan is the winner instead of the sinner. Have you ever thought in your, self, conscious mind that Satan was a believer, once upon a time. Isn't it ironic, when he's out to get you, he believes if "I hang around long enough he or she's mine". When he's on his mission, any means necessary, Satan don't stop until he can prove to God how weak you and I can be, how disobedient, how, its so hard to operate through the fruits is the spirit. He believes if I talk to him or her, if I play with their mind at times, if I could just get them to hang out with me sometime, we'll become the

Change Your Thought Pattern

best of friends. Remember he's a deceiver, it sound like a hit and run situation. Don't be fooled this is why it is important to continue in the faith, never give up on the promises of the creator. If God created the heavens and the earth, ask yourself the question "Whose in Control"? Satan leads us to think that because he was once in that position, in the heavens with God, he wants us to think ,he knows what God is thinking. It's a trick to get us to believe he can present us the real deal. Satan knows how to be patient, convincing, deceiving, and speak the truth in a way that may cause you and I to fall. It is very important for us to know the difference between good and evil, since the fall of man in the beginning. Have it ever occur to you, at times, that good looks bad and evil looks good. The reason why it seems this way at times is because, you have to ask yourself, what is my way of thinking. Am I convince most of the time bad things are happening and less time good things may appear. If 90% of your thinking pattern is negative and 10% is positive, it is obvious that Satan has become your playmate. You will entertain the bad more than the good. Help yourself and others by changing your thought pattern. For Example:

1. If a robber would have changed his thought pattern, he would've held up the bank teller to get money, or taken someone's purse.

2. If the rapist would have changed his thought pattern, he wouldn't have found himself spending the rest

of his life in prison for making or forcing another person to perform a unusual, uncomfortable act that caused them grief and pain.

3. If the husband or wife had change their thought pattern, a divorce could've been avoided, which destroyed the family foundation.

4. If the teenager who was persuaded by friends changed their thought pattern, by not trying uncontrollable substances, wouldn't have died instantly, in the car crash because of drunk driving.

5. If Christians today can believe the word and promises of God by changing their thought patterns, by not allowing Satan to come in, to kill their dreams, steal their ideas and power to obtain wealth, and destroying the promises of God, listening to deceitful lies, we will be most definitely walk in victory.

Changing your thought patterns can be helpful or harmful. If your thought pattern causes you to do things, you're not comfortable with, or bring negativity in your life; it's time to change your thoughts. Changing your thoughts must have done in a timely manner. Every example above could have been avoided if only someone thoughts would have changed. Don't allow people to change your thoughts from the promises of God, remember we are created in his image. When he looks at himself he wants to look good, he's confident, he's wonderful, he walks with authority. My encouragement to you, the next time you're feeling down, sad, or blue.

Remember
THINK YOURSELF HAPPY (LOL)

It's Time To Get Dress

I know at this point you're probably wondering what's this all about, It's time to get dress, well I'm glad you're thinking. When most people think, "time" their thinking, a moment, an hour, a minute, a second, or a certain place, person or thing. When thinking about, getting dress comes to mind; their thinking to cover up. Well knowing when it's time to get dress means you're getting prepared to go to a certain place, or an occasion is about to take place.

Often times as a people, when it's time to go to a certain place, we found ourselves dressing a certain way, with a certain attire. Example: Going to swim, scuba dive, or tanning we often times where, what we would call, bathing suits, swim wear, or deep sea protective equipment. In doing this, we find ourselves, assure, that we will get a tan, exercise our muscles, or discover unexplainable sea shells. Getting dress to go to a party or maybe a family gathering, gets us prepared to get in the right mood, especially the right song, to get the right dance move. We know some way, somehow, to put on the right attire for the right occasion.

Some people because of a lack of knowledge wore a certain attire, to convince others they were saved, sanctified, and filled with the Holy Ghost. But to later find out that, the spirit of Jezebel was a spirit. A controlling spirit, a spirit that went after leadership, headship, the top. Because of a lack of knowledge, people replied; your skirt is to short, your lipstick to red, your blouse is cut to low; not thinking about Jesus was a man that saw the heart of a person, not the attire. He looked beyond the flesh and saw the need. The need of someone's attire can be appealing or offensive.

The appealing side draws attention to those with a positive sense of attitude, the offensive can just be a reminder of a negative individual, who maybe have had a bad experience, or constantly fights with the spirit of insecurities, which basically boils down to fear. Why fear; if you proclaim to be a child of God, of the most high, the almighty, which can do anything but fail, then embrace your salvation. Some people spend the majority of their time trying to convince others, appearing that they have it all together when deep down inside, they struggle with the spirit of intimidation.

It's time to get dress with the spirit of humility, longsuffering, peace, love, joy and happiness and stop covering the truth about who you really are, who you can really be. To dress is to cover; to protect; to present. When Jesus <u>covered</u> a multitude of sin, he recognized that, this can be a good thing, this can be profitable, and this is worth waiting for.

It's Time To Get Dress

When he saw us in our sin, he saw us in the spirit, accomplishing those things he expected out of us. He saw us before time, what we're going to do, say, and experience. The question is how do we see ourselves? How can we comprehend to the things, already designed for us to prosper if we're constantly focused on the negative? When we as a people allow ourselves to focus though spiritual eyes, we'll see things differently, we'll act different, we might just develop a Christ like attitude. It's time to get dress, recognize, and focus on the type of attire we desire to walk in.

If you dress with prosperity, wear prosperity drawing attire, and watch how the spirit of lord move upon those to see you different, offer you substance, because they recognize, you're going somewhere. Don't dress as if you're trying to get attention in all the wrong places, and find yourself with more unnecessary problems than you'll expect.

It's time to know what you want, and want what you know, that's best for you. But most of all; acknowledge God in all your ways, and he shall direct your path. Ask yourself during your prayer or meditation time, how I should dress, what shall I wear, who do I expect to attract. Most times depending upon the mindset of a person, you'll go by what you'll see. Getting dress for the kingdom here on earth prepares us to get ready to go to heaven someday. How do we get dress for the kingdom? Well I'm glad you ask, put on your garment of praise, may a joyful noise, asks your father to create in you a clean heart and renew the right spirit. Only the pure in heart shall see the kingdom someday.

Getting dress with the right attire and the right attitude can maybe get you a promotion, bring wealth, and attract people who need to save. Getting dressed up with expensive clothing doesn't mean you're somebody superior. For some people wearing expensive clothing gives them the mindset that I feel good, I'm beautiful, I'm handsome, I'm attractive, unlike some, this can be a cover up to hide hurt, pain, disappointment and fear. Most people cover pain, hurt, and disappointment sometimes with the right speech "oh I'm okay", "I'm alright", "I'm good", just to stay sometimes under cover.

When a mother covers her new born child she makes sure that her child has the right attire for his or her head, chest, ears, hands, feet, and sometimes an additional blanket, depending on the temperature. She makes sure that the child is well protected, why because she doesn't want her child to become exposed to things that may make her child sick.

Did you not know that our heavenly father sees us the same way? He has given us instructions to put on the whole armor, in order to be protected from the wiles of the wilderness. He wants his children to be aware the temperature of time in our lives. Certain coverings are used for certain situations.

For example:

1. When it's cold outside a sweater, jacket, gloves, and hats are needed.

It's Time To Get Dress

2. When surgeons perform surgeries, certain protective garments must be worn to protect the surgeon from being exposed to germs, infections, or diseases during surgery.
3. When intimacy is taken place, latex should be used to prevent UN expected pregnancy or UN expected stds.
4. When gardeners are gardening protective garments are worn to prevent insect bites, cuts, and bruises from thorns or disturbed wasp nests.
5. Chefs where certain attire to ensure cleanliness, and the prevention of germs spreading to others while preparing meals.
6. When walking or running on hard surfaces, shoes are needed to protect your feet.

Remember whatever your dress code require to defeat the enemy keep in mind "It's Time to get Dress" and put on the whole armour.

Conceal your Weapon

In life we as a people have been taught that a weapon is use to protect ourselves from all hurt, harm, or danger. In most cases if we haven't been taught how to use a weapon not just any weapon, but the certain type of weapon needed when trouble arises, we can do more damage to ourselves than the enemy we're trying to protect ourselves from. Guns, Rifles, Knives, Hooks, and Bolts, explosive devices, chemicals and chains can all be used to protect you or harm someone else.

We know that each of the listed above have been use at some point or another when a situation occurred. Focusing on harming another individual, city, or nation is a demonic force of the enemy to keep human beings in bondage, not working in unity, just to satisfy the greed of the flesh. When someone has been exposed to wealth most of their life, they have no comprehension level to poverty.

Before they allow themselves to become poor or I might say get to a lower class of living, the enemy (the devil) will use them to kill, steal, and destroy in order for them to maintain their wealth level. It is a known fact that children have killed their parents in order to possess the inheritance before time.

Companies have stolen billions of dollars, convincing people who trust their business, to manage their hard earned money to find out later on, that your money was used to invest in other multibillion dollar businesses to make more money, when you only received maybe 1%-2% interest while they pocket the rest. Why is it we can only get interest off of what we deposit in the bank, and depending on how long we allow the money to sit there. Interest off your own money. Wake up it's a give or take "I give you a little interest, if you allow me to manage your money, under certain conditions, if you go below what you put in then I can charge you finance charges, late fees, annual fees, a penalty; do it my way or I close the account you thought you had; Lol it was just a game.

The adversary really knows how to get into the minds of consumers to keep the people blind and in bondage. This world system was not designed by our heavenly father, he gave us life, a life more abundantly, and it's up to us to go after our inheritance he promised us. If our father clearly states are slow to speak and quick to listen, he was letting us know that our mouths can be used as a weapon of mass destruction. Remember life and death lies in the tongue, only speak those things in which they are.

For Example:
1. *If a person is ill and constantly speaks I'm sick, the mind, and body reacts to what you allow to enter in.*

When that person speaks I'm healed the body medically sends messages to the mind to release healing fluid in certain parts of the body to begin the healing process. Evidence will show through scabs, dry skin, and dried blood indicating it's gone, it's over, and you're healed.

2. *If a person speaks constantly I'm broke then money never comes your way because you have except this spirit to enter your mind, which the mind controls the body, you will never exercise your gifts, or hidden talents God gave you when he created you. Instead, speak money come to me, money has my name on it, Abraham Lincoln, George Washington, and Franklin Roosevelt did. When paper declares pay to the order of, it can only be paid to the person whose name of whom it is written to. Most times if you can see it, then declare it, claim it, and then possess it.*

3. *Once upon a time I spent hour's maybe days at the dermatology office trying to resolve the fact that, it has it be a treatment for keloid skin. Well after getting tired and restless, sitting at Jackson Memorial in fear of the pain, because of the different procedures performed, God always had an undercover angel in disguise to assist me along the way.Until one day sitting there I developed a mindset that, you know what, "I can do this". I can sit behind the desk someday*

> *helping people with health issues, then to discover seven years later I perused the field of a Medical Support Assistant; why because I saw it, claimed it, and posed it. Concealing your weapon means to hold on to, protect it, cover it. A weapon is something that protects you. It's all in how you use it.*

In life we must understand that if your creator has given you something to fight with, to protect you, then you should consider how I should handle what was given to me as a protector. The adversary (the devil) needs to understand that we as a people of God have a protector, comforter, and concealer. All three are needed to hold on in these last and evil days. So please by all means hold on, trust God, have faith, be patient to your instructor, mentor, leader, guider, or your unconditional loved one himself Jesus, El Shadier, Jehovah, Aloha; whatever and whomever you want him to be, in your life. Concealing a weapon requires you to protect that which is giving to you for your protection.

> Remember in the beginning the word was spoken "Let there be", and it was. Conceal your life with the word of God and surely you will be protectected. The word is a weapon to remind satan "It is written".

It Was All In The Plan

Did it ever occur to you that, why did I go through being raise in the ghetto, loosing parents at a young age, being molested or almost, being kidnapped, foster care, getting divorced, bankruptcy, unsuccessful relationships, false accused, prison time, ministry struggles, or any of the uncomfortable hurting things that an individual can go through which was really not your fault. Well to help you understand from a spiritual point of view, we must understand as a people that our lives are predestined "pre" meaning before which means before time. If our God is the Alpha and Omega meaning the beginning and the end, then this means that God already has predestined our beginning and end of our lives.

The question is, since I was born and gone through the things I've gone through at this point in my life, where do I go from here. Well to help you better understand when you are called or chosen to do Gods will, some things were destined, in the plan, for you to go through in order for you to get to the next level or dimension that God has planned for your life. Remember we have been bought with a price, and Jesus paid the price of being wiped, talked about, beaten, and dying so that we today can have a chance to the tree of life, for all those that believe that he died and rose, to understand that his spirit lives today.

It was in the plan that in order for you to be made whole, especially when, you find it hard to keep Gods commandments, that you went through the divorce to help others better understand how important marriage is unto

God a holy matrimony, and covenant. It was in the plan during your childhood you were almost for some and was for others molested, and made it through not being killed in the process of a sickening act of a demonic spirit, taking advantage of your innocence. It was in the plan, you lost your parents and found yourself in a foster home or shelters around others who couldn't understand, "why am I here" "where's my family"; which help you to understand that after you left such a place and found a life for yourself, why you have such mercy on runaway children who can't communicate with their parents in a way that they can express themselves more freely to want the attention of more love.

It was in the plan that you experience going through an unexplainable illness, after being healed, you can help others to understand, that life is so precious and that having your health and strength, plays an important role in reaching the destiny God has ordained you to reach someday. It was in the plan that God allow Satan to show you that even though the temptation of the enemy aroused up against you, that you were still protected, because he knew that you were Gods child, and he could only go so far.

Which means that someday you will be used by God to help other hurting individuals that carry that burden and pain today, trying to get through life, and letting go the pass? It was in the plan that you escaped being kidnapped; you survived, and persued your life, encouraging others to be more cautious, not to get so easily acquainted with strangers that may harm you. It was in the plan that you lost your parents at a young age not understanding, that parents are supposed to be around to take care of their children, to later realize that you can teach other children that they must obey their parents, for this is right in the sight of the lord, and to hold on to the teaching of what you were taught in order to get through life when challenges come.

It was in the plan that you tried to open your own business, and found yourself with not enough resources or support to get the business off the ground, to later discover that until you understand that putting Gods business first in your life, will take you places, you've never dreamed of, and allowing the holy spirit to lead and guide you to the right place, at the right time, to give you what you need to jump start your business to be a blessing to others.

Remember Gods way or no way. It was in the plan that you experience having children out of wedlock, being disobedient, not being patient to family planning, experiencing the struggles of a single parent, having unprotected sex, fighting bacteria that the human body doesn't deserve;

discovering now, that after God has healed you, kept you, saved you, shield you, you can now teach and preach your testimonies to others, that if you wait on God, life is worth living, and he can show you great and mighty things.

It was in the plan that you finally met that special one that you found yourself wanting to spend the rest of your life with and you experience and un expected death which caused you some grief, sorrow, pain of a broken heart, when later on you'll discover it was all in the plan to continue Gods will for your life. Others that watch you will become strong by your endurance, your strength, your perseverance, your struggles, even when you find yourself at times crying inside.

It was in the plan that you know that God has called you to a ministry to carry out the plan for his people, and at times you find yourself questioning God was this really you lord, that spoke to my spirit that day and told me to go and preach this gospel, so that those that are blind, and in captivity, of not knowing the truth, whole truth and nothing but the truth, and help them understand this is a spiritual faith walk.

It was in the plan that those that came and gone were only there for a season in order to keep the spirit moving, if some don't go others won't grow. It was in the plan as a leader you had to go though the backbiting, the covertness, the lying, the cheating, the stealing, false accusing, the form of godliness, the deceiving, all that can occur to stop the plan of God. Not knowing it was a set up to be blessed up. It was in the plan that you did prison time, to move out of your comfort zone in order for you to hear God when he speaks, and move when the holy spirit says move. When you're chosen, hand picked, picked out, picked on, its because you're walking with explainable power.

Sometimes in life we may not understand Gods plan for our lives, but if we continue to seek him diligently, acknowledge him, and ask, he will direct our path. And in the end you will understand,

"IT WAS ALL IN THE PLAN".

Use Your Tools Naturally and Spiritually

The word tool is best described as a device or implement; one held in the hand, used to carry out a particular function. When you have been chosen by God and have been gifted through your hands it is imperative that you carry out your assignment. Most people don't realize, we were born with hands for a reason. It may sound strange but if your hands are used what they were created to do, you will find very interesting things can happen in your life.

In the natural and spirit hands are use for varies reasons such as creative writing, painting pictures ,holding devices and objects, lifting and delivering items, typing memos, letters and documents, cooking foods, cleaning, while spiritual hands are use for touching while anointing someone with blessed oil, waving and clapping while praising God producing an atmosphere of joy.

For example: (In the Natural) in order for a carpenter to perform special building projects he must have the right tools in order to complete the job. Now if the carpenter has the right tools and only carry the tools in a tool box, just to say, I have a nice set of strong tools, then to discover, if I don't put these tools to work or make use of these tools, the project will never get complete. This is where a lost takes place.

For example: (In the spirit) in order to fulfill your calling in the gift of your hands, when a situation occurs for you to use your hands for whatever particular situation, you must know what tool to use. Most times when Jesus touched and healed someone the power of healing was transferred to that person to be healed. Once that person was healed, then Jesus now expects that person to perform the same duty with someone else that maybe sick, so that the healing continues from person to person.

First if we believe that we can be use to lay hands on the sick as a point of contact and believe, they shall recover then we will begin using the tool of Faith.

Testimony:

My grandmother Beatrice Harris suffered a growth on her neck maybe the size of a walnut, located on the top of her collar bone, knowing and believing that one day, this growth on her neck will be gone without a surgeon removing it. When people thought she was crazy not to have that removed, she decided to remind people of the goodness of God. After several years of the stiffness in her neck from the growth she spoke with her son James Harris who was in prison at the time, seeking God for himself, knowing and believing also, God can do anything but fail came home one day from prison, asking his mother "what's wrong mom with your neck"? She then explained to him that she didn't know, she thinks the arthritis have caused this growth to develop on her neck . So James then said, to his mother "Mom you taught me from a child to pray and believe" and she said yes, that's right, with tears in her eyes she knew her son had an encounterment with the lord. So James said "Okay mom I'm going to touched your neck and if you believe and I believe and your granddaughter is a witness lets begin to pray". After James rubbed his moms neck she begin to cry and began thanking God for her healing. After days had gone by the growth begin to shrink, and shrink, and the stiffness slowly begin to disappear and today the growth is totally gone with no stiffness. "Wow"

    I witness from a child this miracle right before my eyes that when my uncle used his tool of faith and my grandmother used her tool of faith the both of them touching and agreeing and believing, they got the job done. I found that before her son left to go to prison he was living a certain life style that was displeasing to his mother but when he came home and allowed God to use him in such a way that now his mother can see the manifestation of Gods glory in his life here on earth, and that her prayers were not in vain. Parents! please continue to seek God and pray for your children, no matter what the situation looks like, continue to use your tool of faith. Remember having the tool is one thing, but using your tool is another; faith without works is dead.

When using your tool of the word such as "No weapon formed against me shall not prosper", "I can do all things through Christ that strengthens me", "Man shall not live by bread alone, but by every word that proceeds out of the mouth of God", sends a signal to the devil that, I understand who I am, whose I am, and the Great I AM, which brings your adversary into captivity not to seek you.

The adversary recognizes his tools, and that if he can get us to not use our tools we will be defeated. His tools are used In our everyday lives such as the tool of envy, the tool of jealousy, and the tool of hatred. When he sees that he can't get much accomplished with his tools, unless, he gets permission from God, he then puts his tools on display, and as Christians some of us picks his tools up and use them against one another.

> For example: Sister Whispering Watermelon and Brother Want-To Do –Right, forms at rap session after every church service discussing how well another faithful brother and sister are doing in their marriage. All they can see material wise their blessed, not knowing behind the scenes they maybe faithful but their ordinary people like you and I. They have gone through and sometimes experience worse situations than others. But sister whispering

watermelon and brother want-to-do-right becomes very jealous and envious because while pressing their way to every church service it's always a struggle, the devil always tends to show up just before going to church; not to mention the fake smile that's used while worshiping God because their minds are so cloudy with what the true worshipers are receiving from God.

Now they become bitter and find excuses why they can't attend service as they started out when supporting the ministry first begin in their lives. It's obvious to see the devil has put his tools on display to be used by someone whose mind is no where on God, but wanting what God has for someone else. As believers we must be careful not to become envious, or jealous of any of our Christian brothers and sisters.

This act of the adversary can cause the people of God not to come together as one. He recognizes the power of oneness, unity, and togetherness. He knows that the fruits of the spirit which is love, peace, joy, happiness, and longsuffering will get us to a place in God. So the next time you become angry, envious, or jealous of someone that God is blessing,

"Check your Tool Box", (your heart), you might be holding the wrong tools.

Fire That Burns For The Good

Most people when they hear the word fire, their minds go into a mindset of a loss, a death, or a careless individual. In knowing this, until the situation is analyzed, fear begins to set in. The reason fear sets in, is because, the expectation of the outcome is unsure. Fires are started most times accidental or by an individual who enjoys destruction.

Now, one might ask who enjoys destruction, well anyone that enjoys destruction has mostly likely experienced a intentional loss by someone else. Often times we hear the term "if you play with fire you will get burned" meaning, if you indulge with something or someone bad, bad will come back to you. In most cases, because of individuals that feel that they can do bad to others and get away with it they continue to do bad to others, until bad comes back to them, then that's when realization kicks in reminding them of another saying "what goes around comes around", meaning, do it to me, then I'll do it to you.

Well **"A FIRE THAT BURNS THE GOOD"** simply describes a selfish, unkind, ungrateful, individual that cares about nobody but themselves and what they can get out of a good person. This spirit is best described as the Jezebel spirit. This spirit can be operated through a male or female. This spirit operated mostly to bring down good leaders.

Because of the name Jezebel was given to a woman, most people feel that women that act out a certain displeasing way is considered a Jezebel. When we look at people in life, instead of looking at the person, look at what spirit that person is operating through. Have you as a good person have tried to do nothing but good by people, and all you receive in return is something bad. Why as Christians we feel, why is this happening to me, why should I have to go through this? If you can understand in a more spiritual way, then maybe God can reveal to you why.

Through all things give thanks, so that you will come out victorious. In order to grow, some things must die. As believers we must die to the flesh daily. Just in case you don't understand, dying to the flesh means giving up some, things that don't benefit you, things that give you headaches, heartbreaks, things that can always keep you feeling in control knowing they can be just setbacks.

Example 1: Giving up a bad relationship can cause you to grow and blossom in areas you thought you could never succeed in. It can bring forth more love you thought you never had. It can also allow you to help others who maybe been through the same thing you've gone through.

Example 2: Giving up bad eating habits can help maintain a healthier lifestyle, save you money, and stay out the doctors office.

When we hear the term "I'm hot; he made me hot; or she made me hot" we often receive the mind, set, that, that individual may be mad or angry. Now a good person tends to put up a defense, mechanism, and prepares themselves not to bother that person. As believers we must be mindful that when the devil is in operation; don't turn up the heat. Remember; mama use to say, "You play with fire, you might get burned". Heated conversations between relationships should be diffused quickly, in order to keep the adversary from coming and separating unity.

When we allow the wrong fire to get inside us to say terrible things toward each other, it holds us back from Gods promises. Remember we're created in Gods image; would you look in the mirror and hurt yourself? Well if you do, maybe you don't understand everything God created is good. Don't get upset with yourself then go around becoming a fire starter.

Example: Mr. or Ms. Channel 7 goes around and collects news. But the only news collected was what he or she heard, never facts, never actually seen the news he or she collects; just what he or she heard. Sounds like a gossiper. Once Mr. or Ms . Channel 7 spreads the news and it gets back the wrong way, then here comes the firefighters who can't put the fire out, because of how large the fire has gotten, then good people accidently gets hurt from the explosion.

If you know you are a good person, when someone gets in your presents trying to start a fire "Run Like Hell" your life is more meaningful then getting burned by a fire starter. A good fire can burn off things in our lives that's maybe holding us back in life. The good fire is commonly described as the anointing. Having an anointing to get things done. It gives our father the glory from who he created. An anointing comes upon you after you've gone through the fire, and came out, without allowing the situation take you under. Remember after gold has been tried through the burning of fire, then its identified as the pure, real thing. So remember

"GO THROUGH THE FIRE BECAUSE IN
THE END, IT'S ALL GOOD".

Unconditional Love

*U*nconditional is an action word that simply means to undo the conditional. Well depending on the mind set of an individual, often times people tend to extend a certain level of love. Meaning, I can only give you, what you give me or a most popular saying "you give what you get". In some cases if we think like that, then we will react like that, but deep down inside we want more.

When most people use the term Love, it can sometimes mean that person maybe lacking the feeling of love, and wants more. Unconditional love goes much deeper than the surface. As believers we must remind ourselves that Christ loves us unconditionally and since we're created in his image he expects us to do the same.

Unconditional love is not always what makes you happy, but denying yourself for others. Christ denied himself with unconditional love, so that we could have a chance to the tree of life. Maybe some people don't understand how precious life is. Can we honestly say to ourselves are we loving ourselves unconditionally, do we remember we've been bought with a price, our savior was wounded for our transgressions.

If a person is willing to lay down his or her life for you to have a chance to better yours, should you take that for granted. Just think maybe I need a reality check.

Example: 1. As a single parent mother or father due to the situation he or she maybe had to make a crucial decision of moving to another state, get out a bad relationship, give up school, or changing jobs just to better the circumstances of their children; displays unconditional love. And in doing this the children developed better attitudes, saw life for what it really was and excepted the successful attitude that "I will make it", I want more out of life, than struggles.

Example: 2 Gary likes peach cobbler desert, but his wife enjoys lemon cake. Gary asks; his wife, honey, what are you cooking for desert after dinner tonight? Ann replies; I don't know yet since you made me mad yesterday, I may not cook nothing. Gary replies; oh well I know somebody who will. Ann while cooking thinks about Gary's comment. Then she thinks about how Gary is such a loving husband in spite the upsetting moments at times, she surprises Gary with a peach cobbler desert.

Question: Was unconditional love displayed? Yes/No

Answer: Yes, because in spite of Gary made Ann mad the day before, Ann continued her wifely duty to submit to her husband.

When we as believers learn to operate through unconditional love we can win every time. Unconditional love breaks barriers between relationships, it provides better communicational skills, it helps us to become stronger in God.

Unconditional Love simply means to go that extra mile. Do things you would not normally do for your spouse, your children, friends even in your work. Unconditional Love is taking a load off someone else. Unconditional love is wanting to see someone get ahead.

Unconditional love means I have to love in spite of. There have been times were showing unconditional love in an abusive relationship becomes difficult.

Sometimes doing and saying things different than the person being abusive can help them realize that if I don't change I will experience a loss. In life Christ allows us to make a choice. In the beginning he gave Adam and eve special instructions.

It was up to their obedience rather the road they took was going to be successful or not. Well you know what happened because of disobedience. We should understand that everything God made is good.

Showing unconditional love to someone that don't love themselves builds a stronger character in you. It helps you recognize how not to be. Your purpose is to help them get to where you're at. Christ unconditional love covers a multitude of sin. As a people if we love unconditionally, healing takes place in us, we prosper in the things of God and in the world. Remember Unconditional Love sets you up to deposit a future withdrawal.

Example: I've been believing God for a ultimate financial windfall but until the season comes; I must continue to treat others with unconditional love before the finances arrive to my account. By faith if I continue to sow financial seeds in secret God will then reward me openly someday.

Testimony: After receiving monies to do one thing, I end up doing another. I picked up the phone out of fear asking a woman of God to please trail me to the gas station to get some gas and that <u>I will pay her back on Friday pay day;</u> I don't have credit cards. When I got off the phone; knowing I didn't want to ask, I then received a phone call right after that from someone I haven't spoke with in years. As we were conversating *they talked about they just got off work and they needed their hair braided. Since braiding hair was a side job for me, I ask the person what do they need. The person replied; "just a few braids going straight back". So in my mind I said "Wow" thank you God, so I told the person okay, come on I'll do your hair. When I hung up the phone, I told God thank you for the woman of God with a giving spirit to help me with no problem.*

The person came by got their hair done and bless me with more than I expected. I believe because the woman of God moved quickly with compassion to be helpful, God allowed the phone call of finance to dial my number and I was able to pay the money back before pay day with the extra I was blessed with. Remember God will test you before he bless you. Remember in order to get promoted you must, "Pass the test".

Showing unconditional love can bring us out of debt. If believers understand that when one is in debt, we're all in debt. Our country are in debt, because of no unconditional love displayed, poor decision making, greed. If we can walk in unconditional love, we can change the world. It will be like heaven here on earth. No poverty, No sickness, No stress, No crime. *Why wait, seek, and ask God to help you walk in unconditional love.*

Seed And Soil

Seed and Soil recognize each other are needed to perform a manifestation of what was planted. In order to gain good fruit, vegetables, flowers, herbs, or a vineyard, one must understand that soil is needed to reproduce a seed. The description of a seed given spiritually can be recalled as a person; for example, the seed of Abraham; which is the earthly decedents living today obtaining the promises of God spoken years before the manifestation   begin.

The seed of finance; recalls, giving tithes and offerings. A seed of life; when one is pregnant with a child, which becomes a fully developed human being within a 9 month grace period. A seed of discord; when someone yields to their flesh causing confusion, while *peace abides. But while remembering whatsoever a man sow, that shall he reap; should be self explanatory.*

The seed understands it has been commanded through the time of creation that it must reproduce when planted in the right soil. Seed understands movement. Soil understands temperature. In our everyday lives if we understand the role of seed and soil we will be more affective when planting spiritually.

Soil is a damp, oil based, fine dirt, which is used for varies purposes; mainly reproducing seed. In the beginning the lord spoke let there be, and it was. Did it ever occur to you that certain seeds such as watermelon, collard greens, pomegrate, tomatoes seeds, etc. were commanded to produce what it was commanded to produce.

For example a watermelon seed knows to produce watermelon and a collard green seed knows to produce collard greens. Everything has been commanded to do what it has been commanded to do. Soil knows how to be use in certain seasons. When soil is damp, soil understands it has been touched with another substance. It automatically gets prepared to receive.

As people of God, we can learn by the elements of this earth how to come together in order to be fruitful. Remember one plants, one waters, but it is God that gives the increase. So the next time you find yourself in a unfruitful drought, remember what you give in life is what youll receive.

"KEEP PLANTING ITS HARVEST TIME"

www.ingramcontent.com/pod-product-compliance
Ingram Content Group UK Ltd.
Pitfield, Milton Keynes, MK11 3LW, UK
UKHW022216230426
12048UKWH00016BA/889